BEFORE
AND
AFTER
THE DOVES

By

Sue C. Bykowski

authorHOUSE®

AuthorHouse™
1663 Liberty Drive
Bloomington, IN 47403
www.authorhouse.com
Phone: 1 (800) 839-8640

Published by AuthorHouse 01/26/2015

ISBN: 978-1-4184-2246-2 (sc)
ISBN: 978-1-4140-8659-0 (e)

Library of Congress Control Number: 2004092134

Any people depicted in stock imagery provided
by Thinkstock are models, and such images are
being used for illustrative purposes only.
Certain stock imagery © Thinkstock.

This book is printed on acid-free paper.

Because of the dynamic nature of the Internet, any web
addresses or links contained in this book may have changed
since publication and may no longer be valid. The views
expressed in this work are solely those of the author and
do not necessarily reflect the views of the publisher, and
the publisher hereby disclaims any responsibility for them.

I wrote my feelings down as a therapeutic recovery and have enclosed them so that women understand and realize that what they are feeling is normal and that some else had the same types of emotions. There is a way out. You have to make the decision and do it. Don't second guess yourself and you and your children's safety, especially on his account.

It is not the desire to leave, but the determination to do so.

Willpower over comes the desire, but the fear will force us to do what we need to do.

Nothing ever comes easy to anyone, especially for an abused women.

With the help and advice of family, friends and professionals anything is possible.

<u>Dedication</u>

I'm writing this book for many personal and social reasons.

I was a victim of domestic violence many years ago, before my eldest son was even born. It was 3 long years before I made the decision to leave my abuser. I have faced many challenges and cross-roads but none have ever been as dramatic and emotionally scarring as the domestic violence.

I really didn't rely on my family and friends for help and support until years later. I conquered my fears and my abuser myself.

But it wasn't easy. I still have flash backs and nightmares of my past. Yet, as the years move on they are not as traumatic any more.

I have reached many milestones in my life as well as in my children's lives. We are survivors.

I have a special best friend who will always be in my heart as well as part of my soul. I can count on him to keep me grounded or for someone to talk to. It is very important to me to have his companionship, understanding, and love. He has been my wall of support, logic, and strength. Whether he knows it or not he is my soul mate.

My friends and co-workers from the past and present have been the boundaries of my protection and strength. My rocks of support.

Leaving the Abuse

Leaving.

This may be one of the most hardest thing a person can do in a relationship. But getting out may be the only way to end the violence. Taking the child(ren) away from a parent and going some where that is unknown and strange, can really put more pressure and strain on one's self. Although the road may be long and look dark and endless, believe me, it can be done.

I vividly remember the day I left my abuser. I packed what I could into 3 trash bags, walked to the gas station down the street, called the police (my phone was ripped out of the wall from a previous fight), walked back to the house, and waited for the police (which seemed like an eternity). When the police finally arrived, I grabbed the trash bags filled with clothes and a few necessities, walked out the door and never looked back. It was so hard to leave my life behind, my job, friends and even family. But, I couldn't let him violently abuse us any more. I had to leave for my kids. Their safety and futures was at stake.

Yes, I won't deny that it was really hard, nor will I question the fact that I had serious doubts about rasing two kids by myself.

Yet, I'm happy to say that I did it! I had a few bumps along the way, but the goals that I had set for myself and achieved out weighed all the fears that I had. To this day, I still have not gone back to him, nor contacted him...it's been 9 years.

I have accomplished so much and my children now live in a non-violent family. Yes, even at the ages they are now, I realize that the decision I made so long ago was for the best.

The bruises are gone, the flashbacks are still fading and the memories are just that, memories. The healing is still ongoing.

But the violence is gone. We now live a better life and have met more milestones than one can imagine.

It can be done.

Healing

It is so hard to believe that there are so many women out there that share the same experience as I did so many years ago. I met a few women in the shelter where I was staying at and I was awed by the similarities in all our stories. Fear and low self-esteem were the two connecting emotions. The light at the end of the tunnel seemed so dull and so far away, that it just seemed unattainable.

After being away from my abuser for a week, the onset of healing started-that light was getting brighter every day. The strength that we gave one another in the shelter made my ordeal begin to lessen. Even though we were only there for a short time, we formed a sort of bond, a sisterhood, a love and understanding for each other, all which helped us to heal.

A healing process that started out painful but slowly, enabled us to become stronger, more supportive and even loving for our own self being.

When we left our abusers we lost everything, especially our freedom.

Now, we manage to rely upon ourselves, begin to live again, support our families and to conquer our fears. The healing may never stop, but someday it will be so much more easier. The reasons will also be a little more clearer, but many question will still go without answers.

Our dreams, our hopes, and our lives will begin again. Stronger than before, as we make sure that the next time there won't be a next time.

Ever Again!

What is abuse?

There are three types of domestic violence. Most people are aware of the physical battering. Yet, there are two more that are just as serious. Sexual abuse and psychological abuse. Even if there is no physical abuse, it doesn't mean that there is no abuse.

Physical abuse - is the physical attacks and the aggressive behavior. It usually starts with small conflicts and can escalate into more serious attacks and regular attacks. It often starts with small bruising to possible life threatening or even death.

Sexual abuse - is the physical attacks that lead into sexual intercourse or other acts that are forced upon by the abuser.

Psychological abuse - is mental violence, which includes verbal, insults, possessiveness, isolation from family and friends, destruction of personal property, and the loss of financial resources.

Domestic violence does and will escalate. It usually starts with name calling and threats and a few punches through a wall. But as it escalates to pushing, slapping and/or hitting fighting back can lead to more serious altercations. If the abuse continues on to a more violent rage, it can lead to more life-threatening injuries like, choking, broken bones or the use of weapons.

So what are the alternatives?

TALK to someone. ANYONE. Family and friends are willing to help. There are counselors, police officers, teachers, clergy/pastor; anyone that you can confide in. Once you make that first step, you can move on.

<u>Myths</u>

- Many partners feel that single parenting is unacceptable, that an abusive partner is better than no partner at all.

- Partners in a marriage relationship believe that they are committed into making the relationship work. Failure to make the commitment work is a failure on one's self.

- A partner may become isolated from family and friends, either by a jealous and possessive abuser, or to hide the signs of the abuser. This is because one may feel like there is no place to turn.

- Alcohol, drugs, and stress may be factors in the abuser's behavior. Don't rationalize that if all is well in the relationship the abuse will not happen.

- The abuser rarely beats the partner all the time. There are "quiet" periods when there is romance. So the rationalization of the abusers actions are that they are "having a bad day," or "letting it out."

- Few women get beaten, they just get slapped around a lot. Once the hitting starts it usually escalates may even leading to murder.

- A women that is abused provoked it and deserves it. No man has a right to hit a women for any reason.

- Domestic Violence is a family matter. No! Domestic violence is a society matter. Abuse is abuse. Society needs to break the cycle now.

- Domestic Violence only happens in low-income families. It can happen to anyone in any inome level.

- It can't happen to me.

You've left Him

You've left him, now what? This is a question that you are asking yourself after you have left him or you want to but don't know what will happen if you do. Well, from my own personal experience I can tell you a few things that you should do without question.

If you have gone to family or friends that's great. Personal support from people who you know and love is what everyone needs. However, make sure that you are safe and out of harms way. If not then go to the police and they will assist you in getting into a shelter for women. The shelters are run by volunteers usually past survivors of domestic violence. They can and are willing to help you. When you are at the police station you can have them call the shelter first so you can talk to one of the counselors there. Then by all means go to the shelter. Why?

Because the first few days are the hardest.

You've just left everything, everyone and you are probably not thinking clearly right now. I know that you are thinking that you've left him for awhile and that he has learned his lesson. So, you think that you can go back to him and that all will be okay.

He'll be nicey-nice for a few days, but it will go back to the same thing, but this time he may use you leaving him against you and the situation could become worse. He may cause more physical harm on you.

So, leave him once and for all and don't look back.

Go to the shelter and clear your head. Then listen and learn.

You are not alone. The shelters offer support groups while you are there. You'll learn what the signs are and what he did was wrong, not you. You will also learn about yourself and your children. There are a lot of women out there that are just like you and I. You will be living with these women day and night and unlike the counselors, you will begin to bond with these women. Talk to them, don't think that you are an outsider. The moral support from those women, who have shared the same kind of fear and pain as you had, will help you to heal and to move on with your life. Understanding that you are the victim will help you to become stronger and more determined not to return to him and to prove to him that you can live without him, even better.

You've been in the shelter for a week or so, you've begun to understand what domestic violence is and that you are not alone.

What is next? You can't stay here forever. Take that energy and start looking into housing. Fill out every application for housing that you can get. There are many different housing authorities as well as several

Federal, State and local Section 8 programs. Ask if the shelter has a housing advocate...talk to them... seek out their help. Remember the sooner you start, the sooner you can continue to rebuild your lives for you and your children. Start saving your money and apply for local financial help if possible. Ask family and friends (when it is safe to contact them), for help, I'm willing to bet that they would love to help. If you feel guilty then tell them you will return the favor once you get your life back in order. You'll be surprised by the support you'll get.

Once you have gotten your housing, you can start to piece your life back together. Make sure that you and your children go to counseling. It really helps the healing to be able to vent out your emotions. Therapy will assist you, realizing that the decision you have made was for the best and that you can be a survivor and rebuild a better life for you and your children. You need to understand that you made a very big and meaningful decision in your life and to continue on with the insight that it is a wise, difficult and an important one. When you begin to put your life back together you will see that there is a different life style out there and that you can live without the physical, emotional, mental and financial abuse.

When you leave your abuser, just remember that you only need to establish safety and security. Everything else will fall into place.

Don't worry about the materialistic things and sentimental belongs you left behind. If you have family or a friend that you know you can trust, let them go get it. But if not, just start over.

You don't need to have constant reminders surrounding you in your new life anyways.

Inner Strength

We all have inner strength, somewhere deep inside
ourselves.
With a little soul searching and reassurance, from
one's self and friends, that strength can be found.
Denial can make the searching more difficult and
causing doubt of one's true feelings.
Time is also essential; it can not be done in one day.
Don't rush or push time faster than it should be, one
can become frustrated and lose all hope.
Friendship–the valve of a friendship can help grasp
deep within ourselves with the trust from that special
person.
But why do we need inner strength?
Inner strength makes a big difference in life.
Embrace it and act upon it.
Draw from it make it grow.
You will love and feel better about yourself.
Respect yourself
Believe in yourself.

Questions of the Future

How many more shelters do we have to live in?
How many more times do my children have to make
new friends and leave the old ones behind?
Will we ever have a place to call home?
Are my children mentally and emotionally scarred?
I can bury my feelings, but what about these innocent
lives.
What are they thinking?
They are so young and impressionable.
I had to leave everything and some times it makes me
so mad and other times it makes me cry.
I can sit for hours and think of what we had to give
up and what he has really belongs to us.
My friends knew there was something wrong, but I
was too ashamed to tell anyone.
I was afraid that no one would believe me, just like I
had a hard time accepting it myself.
Family and friends have been supportive, yet I can't
depend on them too much longer.

Sue C. Bykowski

How much longer do I have to wait until it gets better

for us?

Will I ever be able to take care of my children by

myself?

Or will he be right when he said I was an unfit

mother?

Why do abused women have to continue to keep

hurting even after leaving our abusers?

How much longer do I have to keep running?

What will our lives be like now?

Signs of a Battering and Abusive Personality

The way one perceives another one's actions can be taken in different ways. An abusive partner will show more than three of these signs and the abused will feel like they are being controlled, mentally, emotionally, and even financially. The more signs that are present in the behavior of the abuser, the greater the risk of physical violence. The batter will try to explain their behavior as signs of love and affection, however, it may be way to dominate over the other partner.

➢ Promises to do things, breaks the promise and then states that they never promised anything in the first place.

➢ Causes a big scene or commotion in a public place or at a family gathering. When confronted about it later, states that you are exaggerating and making the whole thing up.

➢   Tries to convince you that you need a psychiatrist. But he is fine.

➢   States that you are always imagining things.

➢   Hits you then asks how did you get hurt.

➢   Asks you why you are always upset.

➢   Tells you to make a list of all your faults. He'll help you to improve on your character flaws.

➢   States that you are upset when you are not.

➢   Promises to help when the kids or you are sick and doesn't.

➤ Expects you to stop what you are doing to attend to his needs, but never pays you the same type of attention.

➤ Interrupts you while you are taking, twists you words around, or doesn't listen to you at all.

➤ Show up or not at all when you make plans to go somewhere, then states that you never told him.

➤ When you express you opinion about something he either ignores or laughs at you and calls you stupid.

➤ Always has to have the last word. No matter what.

➤ When you think you finally agree upon something, he changes his mind or does the exact opposite.

➢ His rule is the only rule and you can not change anything that he has already decided upon.

➢ He believes that it is the man's responsibility to make all the important decisions in the family.

➢ Nothing that you do is ever good enough.

➢ Makes you feel that you are not giving 100 % into the relationship.

➢ He dislikes the way you cook, clean and dress.

➢ Never gives a compliment.

➢ Calls you names. (Whore, stupid, bitch, etc.)

➢ You are always on pins and needles hoping that you didn't do or say anything that will get him angry later.

➢ You are afraid to be late by five minutes, because he might get mad.

➢ He gives you the silent treatment and you are left wondering what you did wrong.

➢ Threats to tell Social Services that you are a "unfit mother" and that you shouldn't have any children.

➢ He tells you that you can't survive without him. That you will never leave him.

➢ He gets jealous if you talk to other people especially other men. Thinks that you are cheating or going to cheat on him.

➢ Calls you all the time to "see how you are doing."

➤ He does all the shopping afraid you won't get it right or that you will waste all his money.

➤ Tells you don't have to work that he will take care of you.

➤ Picks out what you are to wear, states that he knows what makes you look good and presentable.

➤ Drives you to and from work so that your male co-workers won't get any ideas.

➤ Encourages you to take drugs and drink with him so that you both can share the same high.

➤ Makes all the financial decisions, you don't even know where he keeps the checkbook.

➤ Makes you show him every receipt so he can see how you spent his money.

➢ Spends money any way he chooses, but blames you when there isn't any left.

➢ Lies to you and tells you that he didn't get payed what was owed to him or that he lost his check on the way home.

➢ If you ever left him he would kill himself and it would be your fault.

➢ If you left him and took the kids, he would find you and kill you.

➢ Nothing is ever his fault. He is the victim.

➢ Makes you do things sexually that you are not comfortable with.

➢ He expects you to be the perfect companion, mother, wife.

➢   He has a blind rage and doesn't remember afterwards.

➢   He can be described as a "Dr. Jekyll/ Mr. Hyde" Personalility.

➢   Breaks, throws away or sells your possessions.

➢   Threats to harm or kill you.

➢   Uses physical restrains on you (holds you hands down, pulls you by the hair, etc).

➢   Has had past domestic violence with an ex.

<u>My Children</u>

As I'm writing this, I am watching my two precious little one's sleep. I wonder what they are dreaming about.

Are they pleasant thoughts and dreams? Or are they dreaming about the abuse that they saw and heard?

How much will they remember? If they remember at all.

I ponder the thought if they will be abusive themselves someday of will I be able to end the domestic violence? I strongly and most passionately believe I've done it, but only time will tell.

How can anyone let innocent children learn and live with such a harsh and insecure environment and expect them to be okay in today's society? The experts think they have all the answer, but do they? Then why can't they (experts) answer my questions?

My emotions are in such a turmoil because I can't predict the future for my children. So, I can't help but to wonder if I have been successful in helping my children for their future. I know my pain will last for a long while, but what about theirs? I have and can find outlets to help me heal. They in a sense can not.

They are too young right now to write, to draw, and to ask questions to get an understanding of their feelings. They are too young to talk, so they can not verbally express their true emotions.

I honestly hope they are not hurting inside. I also feel confident that I've taken away a lot of the hurt and the hate that they may have felt by leaving my abuser whom they loved.

As a parent, I understand there will be days of scrapped knees and elbows, many hard falls and a few broken hearts. Hopefully, the domestic violence will only be heard and read about as a history lesson in future generations. Theirs.

What more can I do? At times I feel so weak and helpless, sad and alone. Confused and defeated. But my undying love for my sweet little ones is so much more greater than anyone can imagine. When I look at each one, I can feel the love pour from me, reaching for them, embracing them. If you ever loved someone with all your heart and soul, you know that special feeling I'm talking about. And you know how good it makes you feel and how strong it is.

When my children wake in the morning, I know it will be another day to heal, another day we become stronger as a family and as individuals.

But for now, sleep my children, have nothing but pleasant dreams.

Mommy is here and I LOVE YOU with all my heart and soul...FOREVER.

__Take a Step__

He's finished demeaning you, slapping you, and throw things.

He's left you alone to go "cool off." But for how long? When will he start up again? How much more can and are you going to take? Don't take any more!

Leave - Now!

Take your children and go to a safe place. The police, a trusted family member, or a friend are willing to help you.

Yes, it is more difficult to do than to say but why should "he" abuse you day after day for reasons you may not even know. Yes, he probably does love you but violence is not the way to show someone. If you are afraid he'll track you down, don't worry; he can't when you go to a shelter.

What about the children?

You don't want to take them away from their father. You don't want to break up the family. He broke up the family long ago with the domestic violence.

Kids are very smart, they may not be in the same room when he is hitting you, but they do hear the yelling, screaming and the crying. They could be imaging things that are a lot worse. They may be thinking that they are next.

It will be the hardest decision of you life, it will affect the whole family, but after a few months, you'll become proud of yourself for your achievements.

This is the beginning of independence, freedom, and a "non-violent" life for you and your children.

All the television ads, articles and books only encourage you to make the first step, that first phone call. Only you can take and make the steps towards that new beginning that you and your children deserve.

Appreciate the Day

Time is passing by...faster and faster each day.

There doesn't seem to be an ending of how long it will continue.

So, how does someone fulfill and experience everything that life has to offer in such little time that we have?

There is only one real way to be able to answer this question.

By dealing with life and it's experiences "One Day at a Time,"

without rushing through-enjoy the day but with meaning.

Why should one go through life rushing about in a hurry to do this and that, only to get nothing really accomplished, with no meaning nor understanding of how and what has been achieved for that day?

Life is suppose to be enjoyed, so that one can understand what life is about and to interpret the meaning of our lives.

There are many roads and paths that can be taken in
life, yet there is no correct one to take.

The footpath chosen is the one for you, because you
have made the decision to go that route towards your
destiny.

No one else can tell you how to live our life. Only
suggestions may be offered in helping you in over
coming obstacles and problems.

Therefore, there are no wrong nor right decisions, just
like there are no guaranties for your future as well as
anyone else's.

Alone

Footprints are making their marks upon the sand.

Turning around there is only on pair (mine).

Heavy shoulders, a deep sigh, a lonely tear in my eye.

Alone.

A feeling that people don't like to experience.

But a feeling that can hurt someone if the don't

accept it.

Loneliness–I feel scared and unwanted.

"How can I stop this feeling"

I don't like to be alone.

People stare at me when I'm by myself.

I feel so incomplete-is there something missing that I

cannot see.

I feel like society had rejected me.

Well, I don't care.

I don't need anyone.

But deep in my heart I do.

Tears slowly fall from my eyes.

I hate being alone.

Sue C. Bykowski

I wish someone was here.

Just to talk to, someone to listen, someone I can listen to.

Companionship-the company of another person.

I continue on in the sand. I still see only one pair of footprints behind me.

There is only my own, for I'm alone.

Wait...over there...I see someone sitting on the rocks, just a few feet away.

They too are alone, just like I.

I think I'll walk over and say "Hi".

We all need a friend.

For being alone can truly hurt someone emotionally as well as mentally.

It is not hard to make friends when you have a lot of them.

It is easy because it comes naturally to you.

But the next time you see someone alone, stop to think for a minute.

Do they look like they want to be alone or do they need a friend?

Why not go over and see.

You just may be that friend that they need.

Ocean Therapy

Seagulls are flying high over head.

Waves are calmly hitting the shoreline, with small white caps disappearing into the beige colored sand and the royal blue waters.

Quiet...Quiet...Calm.

The ocean has a mystical wonder about itself that seems to draw people out of their misery.

Momentarily, relieving them of society's madness.

Close your eyes. Take a few deep breaths. Can you feel it? Can you feel nature's therapy working within you?

Feel the calmness, go with it...don't fight it or try to understand it.

Let it work, work with it.

Now, slowly try to understand what is going on inside yourself.

Ask yourself—what you want to know—but don't expect an answer right off.

The reply that you will receive is understanding of what is to become...acceptance.

Accept what is going on in your life. It may hurt and confuse you, but it is meant to be that way. The confusion of understanding what is meant to be.

Look above...see those seagulls flying high above you—they look so content and relieved don't they?

They don't seem to have a care in the world. Well, they do, they too have a problem to deal with...nature's cycle.

Now, look at the ocean, calm isn't it? It took millions of years for it to be the way it is now.

However, the human race is slowly destroying it.

Never less, it is still there for you, giving to you the gratitude and serenity as well as a sense of relief.

A place to mediate.

Close your eyes and breath the salty air, listen to the waves slowly approaching you, feel the worries and distress leave you.

Sue C. Bykowski

Washing out into the sea.

Feel the difference when you first arrived to your quiet

and everlasting friend.

You now have your sense of reality back with you.

You feel good about yourself once again and you may

even have a smile. There is only one thing you forgot

to do...

Thank your faithful friend for just being there when

you needed it the most.

Safe at Last

We are safe my children.

No more harm.

We now have a place where we can call our own.

No more running.

The fear has subsided.

Life is new for us.

No more violence.

No more hitting.

I love you more than ever.

I know that you may miss your "Daddy," but my love

for you is stronger than his and I had to take you way

from harms way.

Some day in the future, you will understand and

realize what I did was right for all of us.

It is time for you kids to enjoy playing, making

friends, and to live in a non-violent home.

The worst is over now, no more fear, for we are all

safe at last.

Checklist

Think about how you are being treated and how you treat your partner. Remember, when one person scares, hurts, or continuously puts down the other person, it is abuse.

_____ Tells you that you are nothing without them?

_____ Blames you for how they are or act?

_____ Insults your accomplishments and goals?

_____ Makes you feel like you can't make a decision?

_____ Prevents you from doing things that you want to do? (i.e. spend time with family and/or friends?)

_____ Uses intimidation or threats?

_____ Uses drugs and/ or alcohol as an excuse for saying hurtful things or abusing you?

_____ Pressures you sexually?

_____ Makes you feel like there is "No Way Out" of the relationship?

_____ Keeps you from leaving during or after a fight?

_____ Leaves you "somewhere" after a fight to teach you a lesson?

_____ Do you feel like no matter what you do, your partner is never happy with you?

_____ Do you believe that you can help your partner to change if only you changed something about yourself?

_____ Do you feel scared about how you partner will react to something that you did? Especially if it is something that you did wrong?

_____ Do you constantly make excuses to others about your partner's behaviors?

_____ Do you try not to do anything that would cause a conflict or make your partner angry?

_____ Do you always do what you partner wants to do instead of what you want to do?

_____ Do you stay with your partner because you are afraid of what your partner will do to you or themself if you leave them?

IF ANY OF THESE ARE HAPPENING TO YOU IN YOUR RELATIONSHIP; TALK TO SOMEONE. WITHOUT SOME HELP THE ABUSE WILL CONTINUE AND MAY GET WORSE!

What should you take if you are leaving him?

- ☐ Social Security cards for yourself and children.

- ☐ Birth certificates, Passports (yours & your children)

- ☐ Driver's license, Public Assistance card (if you have one)

- ☐ Bank books, savings, money, bonds-anything financial

- ☐ "His" social security number (it will become useful later for legal reasons)

- ☐ Clothing, and toiletries (if you can)

- ☐ Medications

- ☐ School & Medical records

☐   Divorce papers (if they apply)

☐   Housing paperwork (lease, mortgage with loan number, deed)

☐   Address book

☐   A favorite toy or two for the children (so that they have something that is familiar)

If you <u>plan</u> to leave you abuser, try to pack in advance and give them to a trusted family member or friend for safe keeping, until you need them.

State By State

Many of these numbers accept collect calls.

Alabama - (334) 832-4842   Alaska - (907) 586-3650

Arizona - (602) 279-2900   Arkansas - (800) 269-4668

California - (888) 722-2952   Colorado - (303) 831-9632

Connecticut - (860) 282-7899   Delaware - (302) 68-2958

DC - (202) 299-1181   Florida - (850) 425-2749

Georgia (404) 209-0280   Hawaii - (808) 832-9316

Idaho - (208) 384-041   Illinois - (217) 789-2830

Indiana - (317) 917-3685   Iowa -(515) 244-8028

Kansas -(785) 232-9784   Kentucky - (502) 695-2444

Louisiana - (504) 752-1296   Maine - (207) 941-1194

Maryland -(301) 352-4574   Massachusetts - (800) 992-2600

Michigan - (517) 347-7000   Minnesota - (651) 646-6177

Mississippi - (601) 981-9196   Missouri - (573) 634-4161

Montana - (406) 443-7794   Nebraska - (402) 476-6256

Nevada - (775) 828-1115   New Hampshire - (603) 224-8893

New Jersey - (609) 584-8107   New Mexico - (505) 246-9240

New York - (518) 482-5465   N. Carolina - (919) 956-9124

North Dakota - (701) 255-6240   Ohio - (614) 781-9651

Oklahoma - (405) 848-1815   Oregon - (503) 365-9644

Pennsylvania - (717) 545-6400   Puerto Rico - (787) 721-7676

Rhode Island - (401) 467-9940   S. Carolina - (803) 256-2900

South Dakota - (605) 945-0869   Tennessee - (615) 386-9406

Texas - (512) 794-1133   Utah - (801) 538-4635

Vermont - (802) 223-1302   Virginia - (757) 221-0990

Washington - (360) 586-1022   W. Virginia - (304) 965-3552

Wisconsin - (608) 255-0539   Wyoming - (307) 755-5481

Virgin Islands (St. Croix) -   Virgin Islands - (809) 776-3966
(340) 773-9272

Telephone Numbers I Need to Know

Police Department: **911**

Domestic Violence Hotline: **1-800-799-SAFE (7233)**

Counselor: _____

Attorney: _____

Clergy Person: _____

Child Support: _____

Department of Social Services: _____

Other: _____

Other: _____

About the Author

She is a single mother of two beautiful boys. All three are survivors of domestic violence. Both of her children suffer from Bi-polar and ADHD. She has a full time job and at points through the years she worked two jobs to make ends meet. She had managed to obtain a college degree in business and computers. During all of this she also takes care of her father who suffers from Parkinson's disease. She is caring, supportive and will never make time for herself. Her outlet for her emotions was poured into this book. She hopes that this book can touch the hearts of many women out there that endure domestic violence day after day.